The Emancipation Proclamation

By the President of the United States of America:

A Proclamation.

Whereas, on the twenty-second day of September, in the year of our Lord one thousand eight hundred and sixty-two, a proclamation was issued by the President of the United States, containing, among other things, the following, to wit:

"That on the first day of January, in the year of our Lord one thousand eight hundred and sixty-three, all persons held as slaves within any State or designated part of a State, the people whereof shall then be in rebellion against the United States, shall be then, thenceforward, and forever free; and the Executive Government of the United States, including the military and naval authority thereof, will recognize and maintain the freedom of such persons, and will do no act or acts to repress such persons, or any of them, in any efforts they may make for their actual freedom.

"That the Executive will, on the first day of January aforesaid, by proclamation, designate the States and parts of States, if any, in which the people thereof, respectively, shall then be in rebellion against the United States; and the fact that any State, or the people thereof, shall on that day be, in good faith, represented in the Congress of the United States by members chosen thereto at elections wherein a majority of the qualified voters of such State shall have participated, shall, in the absence of strong countervailing testimony, be deemed conclusive evidence that such State, and the people thereof, are not then in rebellion against the United States."

Now, therefore I, Abraham Lincoln, President of the United States, by virtue of the power in me vested as Commander-in-Chief, of the Army and Navy of the United States in time of actual armed rebellion against the authority and government of the United States, and as a fit and necessary war measure for suppressing said rebellion, do, on this first day of January, in the year of our Lord one thousand eight hundred and sixty-three, and in accordance with my purpose so to do publicly proclaimed for the full period of one hundred days, from the day first above mentioned, order and designate as the States and parts of States wherein the people thereof respectively, are this day in rebellion against the United States, the following, to wit:

Arkansas, Texas, Louisiana, (except the Parishes of St. Bernard, Plaquemines, Jefferson, St. John, St. Charles, St. James Ascension, Assumption, Terrebonne, Lafourche, St. Mary, St. Martin, and Orleans, including the City of New Orleans) Mississippi, Alabama, Florida, Georgia, South Carolina, North Carolina, and Virginia, (except the forty-eight counties designated as West Virginia, and also the counties of Berkley, Accomac, Northampton, Elizabeth City, York, Princess Ann, and Norfolk, including the cities of Norfolk and Portsmouth[)], and which excepted parts, are for the present, left precisely as if this proclamation were not issued.

And by virtue of the power, and for the purpose aforesaid, I do order and declare that all persons held as slaves within said designated States, and parts of States, are, and henceforward shall be free; and that the Executive government of the United States, including the military and naval authorities thereof, will recognize and maintain the freedom of said persons.

continued on the back page

All About America

THE CIVIL WAR

Sally Senzell Isaacs

KINGFISHER

NEW YORK

All About America: THE CIVIL WAR
All rights reserved. No part of this book may be reproduced or
utilized in any form or by any means, electronic or mechanical,
including photocopying, recording, or by any information storage
or retrieval systems, without permission in writing from the
publisher.

KINGFISHER
LONDON & NEW YORK

Copyright © Bender Richardson White 2011

Published in the United States by Kingfisher,
175 Fifth Ave., New York, NY 10010
Kingfisher is an imprint of
Macmillan Children's Books, London.
All rights reserved.

Distributed in the U.S. by Macmillan, 175 Fifth Ave.,
New York, NY 10010

Library of Congress Cataloging-in-Publication data has been
applied for.

ISBN paperback 978-0-7534-6514-1
ISBN reinforced library binding 978-0-7534-6693-3

Kingfisher books are available for special promotions and
premiums. For details contact: Special Markets Department,
Macmillan, 175 Fifth Ave., New York, NY 10010.

For more information, please visit
www.kingfisherbooks.com

Printed in China
10 9 8 7 6 5 4 3 2 1
1TR/0811/WKT/UNTD/140MA

The All About America series was produced for Kingfisher
by Bender Richardson White, Uxbridge, U.K.
Editor: Lionel Bender
Designer: Ben White
DTP: Neil Sutton
Production: Kim Richardson
Consultant: Richard Jensen, Research Professor of History,
Culver Stockton College, Missouri

Sources of quotations and excerpts
Page 4, Charlie Aarons quote: *Born in Slavery: Slave
Narratives from the Federal Writers' Project, 1936–1938.*
(Library of Congress).
Page 8, Levi Coffin quote and story: *Eyewitness to
America: 500 Years of America in the Words of Those
Who Saw It Happen.* New York: Pantheon Books, 1997,
pages 182–184.
Pages 10, 11, 17, 26, Abraham Lincoln's quotes:
http://www.abrahamlincoln200.org/lincolns-life/
words-and-speeches/default.aspx
Page 12, Fort Sumter quote by Stephen D. Lee:
http://www.eyewitnesstohistory.com/sumter.htm
Page 16, General Joseph Hooker quote:
http://www.brotherswar.com/Antietam-3.htm
Page 20, Augustus Dickert quote:
http://www.brotherswar.com/Fredericksburg-22.htm
Page 22, General Robert E. Lee quote:
http://www.brotherswar.com/Petersburg.htm
Page 24, General William T. Sherman's quote: *America
in Quotations* by Howard J. Langer. Westport, CT:
Greenwood Press, 2002, page 121.
Page 25, Richmond's Mayor Joseph C. Mayo's quote:
http://www.nps.gov/archive/rich/ri_bats.htm
Page 28, William T. Sherman's quote: book review in
Time magazine, December 12, 1932.

Acknowledgments
The publishers would like to thank the following illustrators for their contribution to this book: Mark Bergin, Nick Hewetson,
John James, and Gerald Wood. Map: Neil Sutton. Book cover design: Mike Davis and Neil Coburne.

The publishers thank the following for supplying photos for this book: b = bottom, c = center, l = left, t = top, m = middle:
© The Art Archive: pages 9tm (The Art Archive/Culver Pictures); 10tl (The Art Archive); 11br (The Art Archive/Culver Pictures);
18bl (The Art Archive/Massachusetts Commandery Military Order of the Loyal Legion and the U.S. Army Military History
Institute) • © Bresslich and Foss: page 13m • © The Bridgeman Art Library: pages 13br (Peter Newark Military Pictures); 14tl
(Photo © Civil War Archive); 14–15b; 16tl (Photo © Civil War Archive); 18tl (Photo © Civil War Archive); 20tl (Photo © Civil War
Archive); 21b (Peter Newark American Pictures); 23ml (Photo © Civil War Archive) • © Getty Images: page 19bl • ©The Granger
Collection/TopFoto pages 1c; 4tl; 4mr; 5tr; 6tl; 7t; 7mr; 8b; 9b; 10mr; 10–11m; 12tl; 13mr; 16mr; 20–21tm; 20–21bm; 21t; 24tr;
24bl; 25t; 25m; 28tl; 29m • istockphoto.com: pages 14tr (David Hallock); 16bl (Duncan Walker); 16bl (Greg Cooksey); 22bl
(Jason Lugo); 26tl (Duncan Walker) • © Library of Congress: pages 1, 2–3, 30–31, 32 (LC-DIG-cwpb_01983); 4b
(pnp/ppmsc.00057); 7b (pnp-cph.3b49644); 8tl (pnp/var.0683); 8m (pnp/cph.3a10453); 11m (pnp/cph.3g11370); 13t (pnp-
cwpb.04719); 14–15tm (pnp-cwpb.01061); 15tr (pnp-cwpb.01560); 15m (pnp-cwpb.01983); 17m (pnp-cwpb.07639); 19m
(pnp/cph.3g10808); 22bm (pnp/ppmsca.12596); 23t (pnp/cwpb.00882); 23r (pnp/ppmsca.13484); 26bl (pnp/cph.3a11366);
26bm (pnp/highsm.04710); 26m (pnp/cph.3g05341); 26tm (pnp/highsm.04713); 27m (pnp/cph.3901834); 28b (pnp-
cwpb.02798); 29 (pnp/cph.3b48118)
Every effort has been made to trace the copyright holders of the images. The publishers apologize for any omissions.

Note to readers: The website addresses listed in this book are correct at the time of publishing. However, due to the ever-
changing nature of the Internet, website addresses and content can change. Websites can contain links that are unsuitable
for children. The publisher cannot be held responsible for changes in website addresses or content or for information
obtained through third-party websites. We strongly advise that Internet searches should be supervised by an adult.

CONTENTS

Introduction

The Civil War looks at the most important event in U.S. history during the years 1861 to 1865. It explains why and how the nation became divided and what happened when its citizens fought one another in the worst battles ever known in the United States. It focuses on the issue of slavery and on the presidency of Abraham Lincoln. The story is presented as a series of double-page articles, each one looking at a particular topic. It is illustrated with paintings, engravings, and photographs from the time, mixed with artists' impressions of everyday scenes and situations.

A Divided Nation

Plantations and slavery in the South

In 1861, the United States faced its greatest challenge. Eleven southern states broke away from the nation to form a new country, called the Confederate States of America. This sparked a civil war, and the nation almost fell apart.

The U.S. government did not think this new country was legal. No other countries in the world thought it was legal. Still, the South formed its own government with a president and an army. Southern leaders formed the Confederacy because they were afraid that the U.S. government would destroy the southern way of life, which was based on slavery.

The Confederacy wanted all U.S. soldiers and government offices out of their country. President Lincoln insisted that U.S. soldiers stay at Fort Sumter, near Charleston, South Carolina, one of the main cities in the South. When Confederate soldiers fired guns at Fort Sumter to get the northern soldiers out, the Civil War began. People had to decide whether they supported the North or the South.

People for Sale

Slave traders shipped Africans to America and made them slaves. Charlie Aarons was a slave in Alabama. He later told a writer about being ten years old and "placed on a block at the slave mart . . . hearing the different people bidding for him, and being finally sold . . . [He] never saw or heard of his parents or brother and sister again and never knew what became of them."

▼ Sometimes slave families were allowed to stay together, as this one was on a plantation in Beaufort, South Carolina.

▶ An 1859 advertisement for a slave sale

NEGROES FOR SALE.

I will sell by Public Auction, on Tuesday of next Court, being the 29th of November, *Eight Valuable Family Servants*, consisting of one Negro Man, a first-rate field hand, one No. 1 Boy, 17 years of age, a trusty house servant, one excellent Cook, one House-Maid, and one Seamstress. The balance are under 12 years of age. They are sold for no fault, but in consequence of my going to reside North. Also a quantity of Household and Kitchen Furniture, Stable Lot, &c. Terms accommodating, and made known on day of sale.

Jacob August.

P. J. TURNBULL, *Auctioneer.*

Warrenton, October 28, 1859.

Printed at the *News* office, Warrenton, North Carolina.

Plantation Lives

Slaves worked in the fields six days a week. Often, older slaves watched the children while their parents worked in the fields. At night, the parents went back to their cabins to wash clothes and cook meals in the fireplace.

AM I NOT A MAN AND A BROTHER?

◀ The Confederate and Union
states. Delaware, Maryland,
Kentucky, and Missouri started as
slave states but then fought with
the free states. West Virginia
started as part of Virginia but
broke away and joined the Union.

Life in the South

Many southern people owned large
farms called plantations. Plantation
owners, called planters, needed dozens of
workers in their cotton and tobacco fields.
Planters bought African slaves to work on the
plantations. Slaves received no pay and had no
freedom to leave. Planters paid a lot of money
for slaves. They also bought food, clothes,
and houses for the slaves. Even with the high
cost of slaves and land, planters sold their
crops for a lot of money and became
rich. A planter's family lived in a large,
fancy house. Most of the slaves lived in
small cabins near the fields.

A plantation
house with
wooden slave
cabins behind it

The Cotton Business

Factories in the United States and
Great Britain needed tons of
cotton to make cloth for dresses,
shirts, and other goods. They paid
well for bales of cotton from the
southern plantations. Slaves
planted cottonseeds in late winter
and picked the cotton in the fall.
By 1860, there were about four
million slaves in the South.

A Growing Economy

Differences between North and South

In the South, slaves worked in the fields and plantation owners grew wealthy. People in the North lived on small farms or in growing cities. Many worked in factories and stores. Were people in the North and South too different to live as one nation?

▲ The Stock Exchange on Wall Street, New York City, the financial center of the North

▼ A busy street in New York City. Horse-drawn carriages filled the streets.

Northern cities such as New York, Boston, and Philadelphia grew quickly as people moved there from other countries to work in their new factories. Between 1820 and 1870, more than seven million immigrants arrived, many of them from Ireland and Germany. They were looking for a better life.

Factories changed the way Americans made goods such as clothes, guns, and farm equipment. Inventors came up with machines to produce goods more quickly and cheaply. Factory workers did not need special skills. They did the same job—such as sewing on sleeves—over and over again.

Trouble over slavery

By 1860, all the northern states had passed laws to end slavery. Most northerners had freed their slaves. Some white leaders in the South also thought slavery was wrong. But cotton was very profitable, and planters needed slaves to pick the cotton as soon as it was ripe.

Industry in the North

In the 1860s, Philadelphia was the leading manufacturing town in the nation. Some of its many factories made cotton and wool yarn, socks, carpets, refined sugar, and parts for ships and trains. Men, women, and even children worked in the factories. Some factory owners became as wealthy as planters in the South.

Industry in the South

The South had few factories and offices—most people worked on plantations or farms. Yet some plantations were very productive: Using a machine called a cotton gin, a slave could prepare 50 tons of cotton in a day! There were also places called mills with machines that turned wheat into flour and trees into lumber for building.

Connecting the nation

The North *was* different from the South, but these two regions needed each other. The South grew cotton and shipped it to northern factories, where it was made into clothing. The factories shipped the clothing back to the South to be sold in stores.

In the middle of the country, new farm towns were sprouting up. Farmers in such states as Missouri, Iowa, and Illinois grew wheat and corn and sent them eastward to be sold in the cities. Meanwhile, people in the new farm towns needed clothing and other goods from the factories. Now the nation started to build betters roads and railroads to move the raw materials and finished products.

▼ The seaport of New Orleans in the South, filled with bales of cotton

▼ This chemical factory in Philadelphia made medicines. The factory burned down in 1884.

▶ A small southern factory that made guns

Transportation

In 1860, most of the nation's railroad tracks were in the North. Trains took goods from factories to towns, where they were sold. Southern planters transported their crops north on ships sailing from New Orleans, Louisiana, and Charleston, South Carolina.

7

Escape to the North
The Underground Railroad

The border between slave states and free states was called the Mason-Dixon Line. It was roughly the border between Maryland and Pennsylvania. Thousands of slaves tried to leave the South secretly and reach freedom.

People called abolitionists helped slaves get to the free states and Canada. Many abolitionists were free African Americans who lived in the North. Others were white people who hated slavery. These helpers formed a network of escape routes and safe hiding places. This was called the Underground Railroad. Slaves crept away from plantations in the dark of night. They hid in forests, attics, or haystacks and waited for a person or a flashing lantern to signal that it was safe to move again.

▶ Slaves hide in a barn while slave hunters look for them.

▼ Harriet Tubman was a nurse and spy for the Union army during the Civil War.

▲ *Uncle Tom's Cabin* was an important book in the 1850s. Harriet Beecher Stowe, an abolitionist, wrote about the horrible treatment of slaves in the South. The book made many northerners angry about slavery. But many white southerners said the book lied about how badly slaves were treated.

The daring Mrs. Tubman

Harriet Tubman was a slave in Maryland. With the help of the Underground Railroad, she escaped from her master and ran away to Philadelphia in 1849. Instead of enjoying the free life, she returned to the South 18 times. Each time, she led slaves out. Slave owners tried to capture her and promised a $40,000 (today's $1.2 million) reward to anyone who did. She helped more than 300 slaves escape.

Hiding in Plain Sight

In 1850, Levi Coffin wrote about helping 28 slaves who had crossed the Ohio River. "They were cold, hungry and exhausted; those who had lost their shoes in the mud suffered from bruised and lacerated feet ... John Fairfield hid them as well as he could in ravines ... and told them not to move until he returned." Coffin sent a funeral wagon to meet the slaves and told them to march behind it. Once past a graveyard, they were led to safe homes nearby.

▶ Helped by free blacks and whites, slaves escaped to the North and Canada.

CAUTION!!
COLORED PEOPLE
OF BOSTON, ONE & ALL,

You are hereby respectfully CAUTIONED and advised, to avoid conversing with the

Watchmen and Police Officers of Boston,

For since the recent ORDER OF THE MAYOR & ALDERMEN, they are empowered to act as

KIDNAPPERS
AND
Slave Catchers,

And they have already been actually employed in KIDNAPPING, CATCHING, AND KEEPING SLAVES. Therefore, if you value your LIBERTY, and the Welfare of the Fugitives among you, Shun them in every possible manner, as so many HOUNDS on the track of the most unfortunate of your race.

Keep a Sharp Look Out for
KIDNAPPERS, and have
TOP EYE open.

APRIL 24, 1851.

Sent back to slavery

Within the government, arguments flared among members of the U.S. Congress. New territories in the West wanted to become states. Northern congressmen wanted all new states to outlaw slavery. Southern congressmen feared that antislavery states would overpower the slave states.

Congress passed a new law, the Compromise of 1850. California was allowed to join the nation as a free state. The territories of New Mexico and Utah could allow citizens to decide about slavery for themselves. Many southerners thought this plan was unfair to the South. They insisted that Congress also pass the Fugitive Slave Act. This law required people in the North and South to return escaped slaves to their owners.

A Fearful Life

Thousands of slaves ran away from plantations each year. Most left alone, not in groups. Most never reached freedom. Some returned on their own. They were too tired, hungry, and sick to continue to the North. Others were captured and put in chains by sheriffs or slave catchers. They were carried back to their owners, who might have beaten them.

Captured at Home

Following the Fugitive Slave Act, professional slave catchers set out to find runaway slaves. Plantation owners offered them $1,000 rewards. A few slave catchers even broke into the homes of free blacks living in the North. They rounded them up and took them South to be sold as slaves.

Lincoln's Stand

The nation is like "a house divided"

The people of the South were scared and angry. Without slavery, their lives would crumble. Many southerners did not want to be part of a nation that destroyed their right to live the way they wanted.

In 1858, Abraham Lincoln ran in the election for U.S. senator for Illinois. He believed slavery was wrong, but he did not push to stop slavery in the South. He wanted to stop slavery from spreading to new territories and states. More important, Lincoln wanted the states to stop fighting about slavery.

During the election, Lincoln gave a now famous speech that borrowed some words from the Bible: "A house divided against itself cannot stand. I believe this government cannot endure permanently half slave and half free." Lincoln's opponent was Stephen A. Douglas. Douglas believed that the people in every territory and state should make their own decisions about slavery. Douglas won the Illinois election.

Meanwhile, problems between the North and South grew worse. People in the North protested as slaves were arrested and sent back to their masters. Some even sent money to help antislavery pioneer John Brown give guns to slaves so they could turn against their masters.

▶ Lincoln's speech during the 1858 election. Douglas is sitting next to him. Although Lincoln lost the election, his views on slavery made him famous throughout the nation.

▼ A painting from 1884 of John Brown on his way to his death

Harpers Ferry

John Brown hated slavery. In October 1859, he gathered 21 men at Harpers Ferry, Virginia. They sneaked into a government gun storage building. Brown sent word to Virginia slaves to run from their masters, grab these guns, and fight for their freedom. None of the slaves joined Brown, and his plan failed. Soldiers captured him and the rest of his raiders. At his trial, he was found guilty and was soon hanged.

AM I NOT A MAN AND A BROTHER

COLES COUNTY FOR LINCOLN

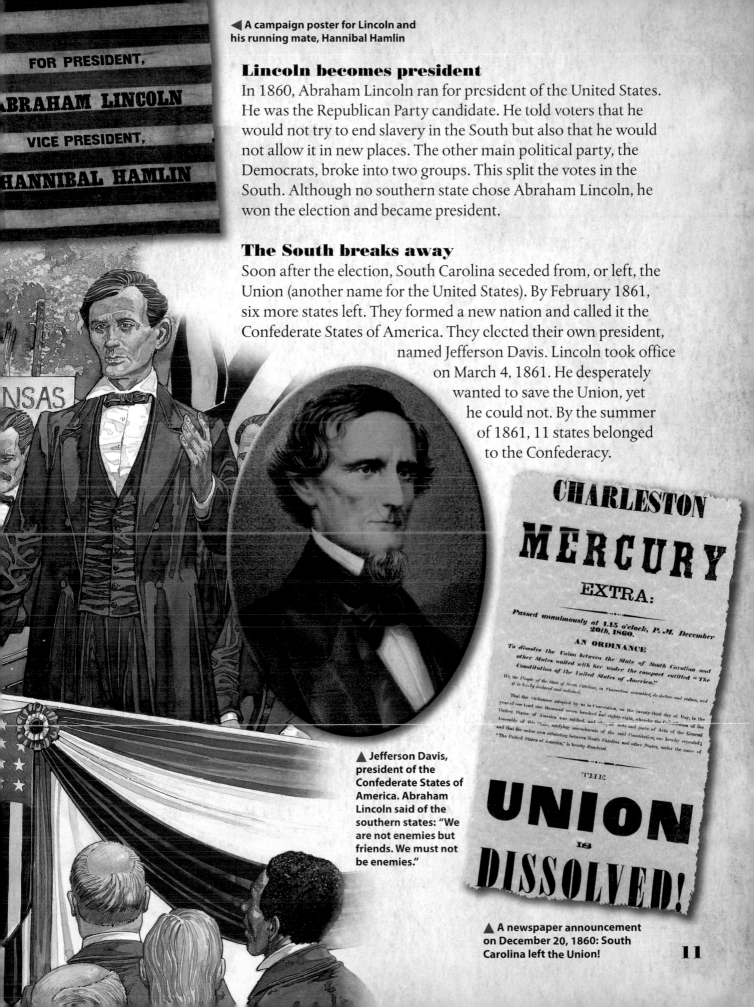

A campaign poster for Lincoln and his running mate, Hannibal Hamlin

FOR PRESIDENT,
ABRAHAM LINCOLN
VICE PRESIDENT,
HANNIBAL HAMLIN

Lincoln becomes president

In 1860, Abraham Lincoln ran for president of the United States. He was the Republican Party candidate. He told voters that he would not try to end slavery in the South but also that he would not allow it in new places. The other main political party, the Democrats, broke into two groups. This split the votes in the South. Although no southern state chose Abraham Lincoln, he won the election and became president.

The South breaks away

Soon after the election, South Carolina seceded from, or left, the Union (another name for the United States). By February 1861, six more states left. They formed a new nation and called it the Confederate States of America. They elected their own president, named Jefferson Davis. Lincoln took office on March 4, 1861. He desperately wanted to save the Union, yet he could not. By the summer of 1861, 11 states belonged to the Confederacy.

▲ Jefferson Davis, president of the Confederate States of America. Abraham Lincoln said of the southern states: "We are not enemies but friends. We must not be enemies."

CHARLESTON MERCURY
EXTRA:

Passed unanimously at 1.15 o'clock, P. M. December 20th, 1860.

AN ORDINANCE

To dissolve the Union between the State of South Carolina and other States united with her under the compact entitled "The Constitution of the United States of America."

THE UNION IS DISSOLVED!

▲ A newspaper announcement on December 20, 1860: South Carolina left the Union!

Horror at Fort Sumter

The Civil War begins

It was April 12, 1861. Southern states hoped for a peaceful split with the Union. Confederate soldiers took over U.S. Army forts and government buildings in the South. At Fort Sumter, South Carolina, Union soldiers refused to leave.

Confederate soldiers fired cannons on the Union soldiers at Fort Sumter. They attacked their fellow Americans! This was the start of a civil war. After more than 30 hours, the Union soldiers finally surrendered and left the fort. The country was in shock. President Lincoln asked men to join the Union army and fight to bring the country back together. Many men signed up. So did boys as young as 12 who lied about their age. Some women dressed up as men and joined, too.

In the South, men and boys joined the Confederate army. The decision did not come easily for many of them. Many people in the South still believed in the Union. Many people in the North hated the idea of a civil war.

◀ **A Union soldier with a Union flag**

Fort Sumter

Fort Sumter sat on an island near Charleston, S.C. Someone who heard the first Confederate shot said, " . . . in this dead hour of the night, before dawn, that shot . . . brought every soldier in the harbor to his feet . . ."

▼ **Confederate soldiers fire on Fort Sumter.**

▶ Morris Island is in the Charleston Harbor. Confederates built a fort with sandbags and logs there. They tried to keep Union ships from reaching Charleston.

▲▼ Two rifles used in the Civil War. They were very accurate and deadly.

▶ The Battle of Bull Run, July 21, 1861

A GREAT RUSH

Cost what it may,

The Nation must be Saved!

36TH REGIMENT
NEW YORK VOLUNTEERS,
Commanded by COLONEL W. H. BROWN.

This fine Regiment, one of the best in the Army of the Potomac, has been an active participant in the engagements on the Peninsula, and particularly distinguished itself during the "SEVEN DAYS FIGHTING," having captured the Colors of the 14th North Carolina Regiment at the Battle of Malvern Hill. The term of enlistment of this Regiment will be out in

NINE MONTHS.
DON'T WAIT TO BE DRAFTED!
THE USUAL BOUNTY GIVEN.
Recruiting Office. No. 17 CENTRE STREET.
BETWEEN CHAMBERS AND READE STREETS.
Lieut. G. H. MOORE, Recruiting Officer.

The Battle of Bull Run

The first battle of the Civil War was like a sports event. It was a hot Sunday afternoon on July 21, 1861. People from Washington, D.C., jumped into their carriages and drove out to a hilly picnic area near Bull Run Creek, Virginia. Reporters from newspapers joined them. From atop this hill, they watched the battle between the Confederates and the Yankees (another name for people who fought for the Union).

The spectators expected a quick Yankee victory. That did not happen. Neither side had much training. By the end of the day, more than 4,800 soldiers were killed or wounded. The tired Union soldiers dropped their guns and ran toward Washington. The spectators realized that this could be a long and bloody war.

▲ A poster to attract men in New York to join the Union army

13

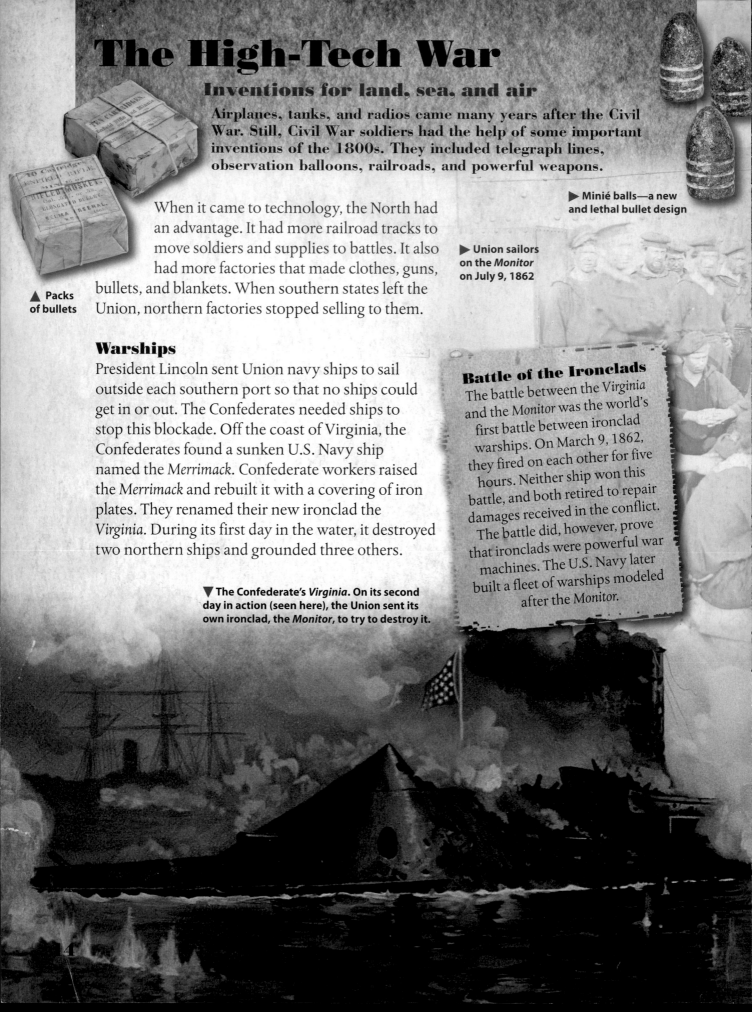

The High-Tech War

Inventions for land, sea, and air

Airplanes, tanks, and radios came many years after the Civil War. Still, Civil War soldiers had the help of some important inventions of the 1800s. They included telegraph lines, observation balloons, railroads, and powerful weapons.

When it came to technology, the North had an advantage. It had more railroad tracks to move soldiers and supplies to battles. It also had more factories that made clothes, guns, bullets, and blankets. When southern states left the Union, northern factories stopped selling to them.

▲ Packs of bullets

▶ Minié balls—a new and lethal bullet design

▶ Union sailors on the *Monitor* on July 9, 1862

Warships

President Lincoln sent Union navy ships to sail outside each southern port so that no ships could get in or out. The Confederates needed ships to stop this blockade. Off the coast of Virginia, the Confederates found a sunken U.S. Navy ship named the *Merrimack*. Confederate workers raised the *Merrimack* and rebuilt it with a covering of iron plates. They renamed their new ironclad the *Virginia*. During its first day in the water, it destroyed two northern ships and grounded three others.

▼ The Confederate's *Virginia*. On its second day in action (seen here), the Union sent its own ironclad, the *Monitor*, to try to destroy it.

Battle of the Ironclads

The battle between the *Virginia* and the *Monitor* was the world's first battle between ironclad warships. On March 9, 1862, they fired on each other for five hours. Neither ship won this battle, and both retired to repair damages received in the conflict. The battle did, however, prove that ironclads were powerful war machines. The U.S. Navy later built a fleet of warships modeled after the *Monitor*.

Going after Richmond

Richmond, Virginia, was the capital of the Confederacy. Union General George B. McClellan thought he could win the war by taking over Richmond. He sent his soldiers by ship to an area close to the city. There he sent up spies in observation balloons to fly over the Confederate camps. The spies reported to McClellan on the size and location of the Confederate troops. After several weeks, McClellan called off his takeover of Richmond. He feared the Union army was outnumbered.

▶ Professor Thaddeus Lowe was the chief balloonist of the Union army. Here in Fair Oaks, Virginia, he observed a battle.

Better communication

The telegraph was one of the most helpful technologies for the Civil War. Invented in 1844, it sent messages electrically over wires. As troops moved, they set up telegraph poles and strung wires between them. Lincoln used the telegraph to send and receive messages with his generals.

Modern Weapons

For the first time in history, modern factories produced war weapons. The latest rifles could fire three shots a minute and reach a distance of half a mile (800 m). Other weapons included hand grenades, flame projectors, and torpedoes that floated in the water and exploded when struck by a ship.

▲ Almost 200,000 African Americans fought in the Union army and navy.

▼ The Union's *Monitor*

Backyard Battles

Death and destruction on a grand scale

This was a personal war. Soldiers marched past front porches and gardens. Plantations and churchyards were turned into battlefields. Homes became hospitals, and backyards became graveyards.

In September 1862, Confederate General Robert E. Lee decided to move the war to the North. He headed his troops from Virginia to Maryland. Although Maryland allowed slavery, it fought for the Union. Lee did not succeed in taking Maryland. Union soldiers found Lee's battle plan written on a scrap of paper. They alerted General McClellan, who took his troops to stop Lee's army at Antietam Creek, near Sharpsburg, Maryland.

▲ A Union army drum

The bloodiest of all one-day battles

The Battle of Antietam was fought by more than 100,000 soldiers on September 17, 1862. About 23,000 in total were killed or wounded. Union General Joseph Hooker wrote about a cornfield that became a battlefield: " . . . the slain lay in rows precisely as they had stood in their ranks a few moments before. It was never my fortune to witness a more bloody, dismal battlefield." The next day, the Union claimed a victory in this battle. Lee took his army back to Virginia.

▼ The Confederacy had several different red, white, and blue flags, such as this one.

▼ Fallen Confederate soldiers at Antietam. As soon as the battle ended, Union and Confederate armies collected their wounded and buried their dead at the site.

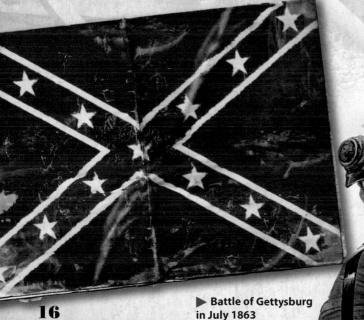

▶ Battle of Gettysburg in July 1863

▼ Part of the Battle of Antietam took place by a bridge over Antietam Creek.

A turning point at Gettysburg

Nine months after Antietam, Lee tried again to take the war to the North. This time he took his troops into Pennsylvania. Union troops, led by General George G. Meade, met the Confederates at the little town of Gettysburg. At the Battle of Gettysburg, about 85,000 Union soldiers fought about 65,000 Confederates. Lee was forced out of the North for good. Once again, the countryside was covered with thousands of dead and wounded bodies.

▼ Lincoln's Gettysburg Address

Changing Generals

After Antietam, Lincoln thought that General McClellan had acted too slowly. He replaced McClellan with General Ambrose E. Burnside. Before the end of the war, Lincoln would choose eight different commanders of his army.

Lincoln at Gettysburg

Part of the battlefield later became a soldiers' cemetery. In a speech given there on November 19, 1863, President Lincoln called the cemetery "a final resting place for those who died here, that the nation might live."

The War's Soldiers

Battle weary, worn, and torn

The war touched almost every family in the nation. Most families had a relative in uniform. They held their breath and prayed that they would not hear bad news from the battlefront.

▲ The cap of a Union soldier

▶ At a Union battlefield hospital. Soldiers received only crude medical care at these temporary hospitals.

A soldier's life could be terrifying one week and boring the next. Soldiers lived in army camps and slept in tents. As they waited for their battle orders, they practiced their marching and fighting skills. In the winter, they chopped down trees and built log walls around their tents to keep out the harsh weather. There were few battles in the winter months, and life became tedious. Soldiers played cards, cooked meals, washed clothes, and wrote letters to loved ones at home.

The wounded

Injured survivors of the battles were quickly taken to makeshift hospitals set up in the camps or in nearby homes and buildings. Doctors and nurses tried to treat wounds without the help of today's knowledge. There was little medicine to block out pain during surgery. People did not yet understand that washing hands before surgery could prevent infections. Doctors and nurses watched diseases spread rapidly from one soldier to another. They did not know how to stop it. In the Civil War, more soldiers died from diseases and unclean medical conditions than from gunfire.

Women as Nurses

Women rushed to hospitals and army camps to take care of wounded soldiers. Clara Barton became famous for nursing care right on the battlefield. After the war, she started the American Red Cross, a group that still helps people in need.

▲ A nurse helping wounded soldiers

Prisoners

Both sides captured enemy soldiers and threw them in prison camps. As many as 194,000 Union soldiers and 214,000 Confederates were taken to prison. A prisoner was likely to die from disease, polluted water, or lack of food. One of the most infamous Confederate prisons was called Andersonville, located in Sumter County, Georgia. More than 12,000 prisoners died in Andersonville. There is a mass graveyard outside the prison. Only one Confederate leader was ever convicted and hanged for war crimes. It was Henry Wirz, the man in charge of the cruel treatment in Andersonville.

▲ Two rows of tall fences surrounded Andersonville. More than 45,000 Union soldiers were crowded into the prison. Anyone who tried to escape was quickly shot.

▶ Union soldiers wore blue uniforms, and Confederates wore blue and gray uniforms. In some areas, it was common for members of the same family to fight for different sides in the war.

Confederate States

By June 1861, there were 11 states in the Confederate States of America. They were: Alabama, Arkansas, Florida, Georgia, Louisiana, Mississippi, North Carolina, South Carolina, Tennessee, Texas, and Virginia. Southern soldiers fought to protect their homeland and to keep their slaves. Northern soldiers fought to keep the nation together and to end slavery.

▲ Union soldiers who posed for a photograph

19

The Home Front
Women, spies, and street fights

The Union was determined to win back the southern states. That meant marching into towns, destroying homes and families, and forcing the Confederate soldiers to give up ground.

▲ A Fredericksburg family waits silently as the battle rages outside their window.

▼ The people of Vicksburg abandoned their homes for shelters in the hillside.

The people of Fredericksburg, Virginia, heard cannons rumble over a nearby bridge. Neighbors spread the word: Everyone should leave town before the battle starts. Augustus Dickert described the day: " . . . soon after the firing along the river began, we saw groups of women and children . . . rushing along the roads out from the city as fast as their feeble limbs and tender feet could carry them, hunting a safe retreat in the backwoods until the cloud of war broke or passed over. Some were carrying babes in their arms, others dragging little children along by the hands, with a few articles of bedding or wearing apparel under their arms or thrown over their shoulders."

Capture of Vicksburg

On July 4, 1863, the Union army captured Vicksburg, Mississippi. Now the Union controlled the Mississippi River, which divided the Confederate states. The Confederates on the western side of the river could no longer send supplies over to their main armies. The Union also succeeded with its blockade of southern ports. The Union's warships captured or sank half the supply ships going to the South. Confederate armies ran short of supplies.

▼ A draft riot in New York

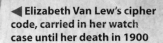
A Master Spy

Elizabeth Van Lew was one of the greatest Civil War spies. She lived in Virginia but worked for the Union army. She visited Union prisoners and secretly helped them escape. She hid messages in the sole of her shoe or in a custard dish. She brilliantly used secret codes and invisible ink to get information about Confederate activities to the Union generals.

Women step in

While fathers, brothers, and sons fought the battles, women took on extra work running the family farms and harvesting the crops. They also made bandages and knitted socks for the soldiers. Before this time, only men were nurses. However, during the war, many women stepped into nursing jobs. Several hundred women dressed themselves as soldiers and fought on the battlefields. Some were found to be women only after they were shot and treated.

▼ Women working in a munitions factory in Connecticut

Helping in Factories

In both the South and North, women also went to work in factories. Some stitched uniforms in clothing factories. Others made bullets in munitions factories. About half the workers in Georgia's munitions factories were African-American slaves.

Drafting more soldiers

When the war began, men and boys excitedly ran off to become soldiers. Most expected the war to end after a few months. By the second year, both sides needed more soldiers. Both had laws that required able-bodied white men to sign up for three years. This was called a draft. If a man did not want to fight, he could pay the government $300 (about $8,000 today), or he could pay someone else to take his place. Many thought this law was unfair to the poor.

Draft Riots

In July 1863, the streets of New York exploded with angry citizens. They shouted that the draft was unfair, especially since rich people could buy their way out of it. After four days of rioting, police and soldiers finally took control of the mob. About 1,000 people were killed or wounded.

Fighting Continues

Both sides grow weary

In 1864, General Lee feared the worst for the Confederates. He wrote, "We must destroy this army of Grant's before he gets to the James River. If he gets there, it will become a siege, and then it will be a mere question of time."

After the enormous losses in Gettysburg, the Confederates never regained their strength. There were battles in Georgia, Alabama, Tennessee, Kentucky, Virginia, and Mississippi, and they held on with all their might. The Union piled on the pressure.

President Lincoln wanted all the states to return to the Union and to bring an end to slavery. He hoped to do both with the Emancipation Proclamation that he signed on January 1, 1863. It said that slaves in any states that had not come back to the Union would be "forever free." The announcement did not end slavery right away. Slavery was still allowed in the border states that supported the Union but kept slaves. Still, Union soldiers carried the proclamation into the South. Many slaves left their farms and joined the Union army. Everyone realized that slavery would likely end if the Union won the war.

Caught on Camera

The Civil War was the first conflict for which we have photographs. There were no action photos. A photographer and subjects had to stand still for several minutes while the camera made a picture. As the war raged on, photos were hung in public buildings. Crowds of people came to see them and felt the pain and horror of war.

▶ Soon after a battle, a photographer sets up his camera and photographic plates to record the death and destruction.

Deadly Dictator

The Union called their new giant cannon the Dictator. Soldiers fired more than 200 huge shells into the town of Petersburg, Virginia. Each shell weighed 225 pounds (102 kg). The Dictator could hit a target nearly two miles (3 km) away. Each explosion sent rocks flying in every direction.

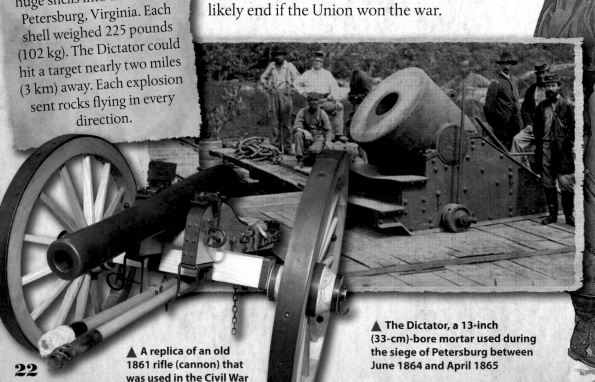

▲ A replica of an old 1861 rifle (cannon) that was used in the Civil War

▲ The Dictator, a 13-inch (33-cm)-bore mortar used during the siege of Petersburg between June 1864 and April 1865

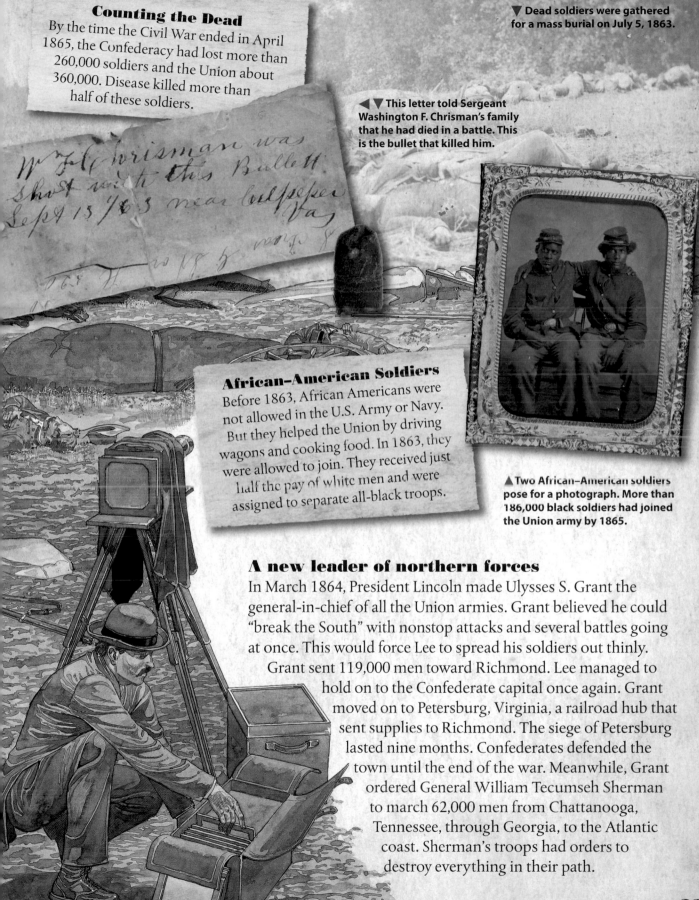

Counting the Dead
By the time the Civil War ended in April 1865, the Confederacy had lost more than 260,000 soldiers and the Union about 360,000. Disease killed more than half of these soldiers.

▼ Dead soldiers were gathered for a mass burial on July 5, 1863.

◀▼ This letter told Sergeant Washington F. Chrisman's family that he had died in a battle. This is the bullet that killed him.

W. F. Chrisman was shot with this Bullett Sept 13/63 near Culpeper Va.

African-American Soldiers
Before 1863, African Americans were not allowed in the U.S. Army or Navy. But they helped the Union by driving wagons and cooking food. In 1863, they were allowed to join. They received just half the pay of white men and were assigned to separate all-black troops.

▲ Two African-American soldiers pose for a photograph. More than 186,000 black soldiers had joined the Union army by 1865.

A new leader of northern forces
In March 1864, President Lincoln made Ulysses S. Grant the general-in-chief of all the Union armies. Grant believed he could "break the South" with nonstop attacks and several battles going at once. This would force Lee to spread his soldiers out thinly. Grant sent 119,000 men toward Richmond. Lee managed to hold on to the Confederate capital once again. Grant moved on to Petersburg, Virginia, a railroad hub that sent supplies to Richmond. The siege of Petersburg lasted nine months. Confederates defended the town until the end of the war. Meanwhile, Grant ordered General William Tecumseh Sherman to march 62,000 men from Chattanooga, Tennessee, through Georgia, to the Atlantic coast. Sherman's troops had orders to destroy everything in their path.

23

Ending in Flames

The fall of the South

By the end of 1864, the South was losing in many ways. Hunger had spread to every farm and city. Thousands of soldiers were dead. Each day, more soldiers dropped out of the army. Then there was General Sherman's march of destruction.

Under Grant's orders, Sherman marched his troops from Tennessee through Georgia and the Carolinas. His goal was to destroy every farm, business, bridge, and railroad line, devastating the South's resources. Sherman warned citizens to run for safety before his troops arrived. Later he wrote about leaving Atlanta: "Behind us lay Atlanta smoldering and in ruins, the black smoke rising high in the air ..." As Sherman marched through the South, many slaves joined his troops.

▲ Union troops tear up railroad tracks.

Presidential election of 1864

The United States had another presidential election in 1864. President Lincoln ran again, this time against General George McClellan. Citizens watched the war to decide whether they trusted Lincoln to win it. By election day, Sherman's army had captured Atlanta and Union rear-admiral David Farragut's navy had won the Battle of Mobile Bay, Alabama. The Union seemed to be winning the war. Lincoln won the election.

▲ ▶ The fall of Richmond, Virginia, on April 2, 1865. The picture on the right shows Richmond citizens returning to find their city in ruins.

Lincoln's Second Term

In his inauguration speech, Lincoln said that both the North and South suffered in the war because they had allowed slavery. Then he asked Americans to "bind up the nation's wounds, to care for him who shall have borne the battle and for his widow and his orphan, to do all which may achieve and cherish a just and lasting peace among ourselves and with all nations."

▲ Lincoln started his second term as president with his inauguration on March 4, 1865, in Washington, D.C.

▶ Before fleeing Richmond, Confederates wanted to destroy anything that the Union might need. A huge fire destroyed the Gallego Flour Mills (shown here) and most other buildings.

Surrender Agreement

For all the bitterness and bloodshed of the war, the end was simple. Confederate soldiers could go home, leaving their guns and other military equipment for the Union to collect. Lee asked if his soldiers could take back their horses to work on their farms. Grant agreed. He also sent food out to the hungry Confederates before they left for home.

The Fall of Richmond

As Sherman marched through Georgia, Grant's cannons pounded Virginia. By April 2, 1865, the Confederates had no choice but to abandon their capital in Richmond. As citizens fled the city, Richmond's mayor told Grant's army: "I respectfully request that you will take possession of it with organized force, to preserve order and protect women and children and property." Once people had left, Confederate soldiers set fire to the city's factories and houses.

▲ General Lee signs the surrender papers at Appomattox Court House.

Bitter enemies meet

Most of the South's great cities lay in ashes. General Lee knew it was now time to surrender. He sent a message to Grant. The two generals met on April 9, 1865, in a Virginia village called Appomattox Court House. They sat in the home of a southern farmer, Wilmer McClean. The meeting lasted about an hour and a half and was strangely friendly. First the two generals talked about the days they had served together in the U.S. Army 18 years earlier. Then they discussed the surrender and signed the papers. Some northerners wanted to punish the Confederate soldiers and states, but Lincoln told Grant to bring them back into the Union peacefully.

Lincoln's Last Days

Death of the president and slavery

Should the seceded states be allowed right back into the Union? What price should they pay? Many northerners asked Lincoln to punish the Confederate states, but he wanted to reunite the nation quickly and end slavery.

President Lincoln asked Congress to pass a constitutional amendment to abolish slavery. Congress sent the 13th Amendment to the states in February 1865. By the end of the year, slavery had ended forever in the United States. Unfortunately, Lincoln never saw this happen. He died on April 15.

On the evening of April 14, Lincoln and his wife went to Ford's Theatre to watch a play. John Wilkes Booth crept in behind the president's seat and shot him. Booth leapt down to the stage and escaped out the theater's back door. Members of the audience carried the president to a home across the street. He died the next morning.

A conspiracy

Booth was part of a group who blamed Lincoln for the war. They wanted to hold on to slavery and the Confederacy. The government offered a huge reward to anyone who captured Booth and his gang. On April 26, soldiers in Virginia found Booth and a friend hiding in a barn. The friend surrendered. The soldiers shot and killed Booth. There was a trial for eight other people. Four received the death penalty. The others went to prison.

▶ **Tickets to Ford's Theatre for the night of Lincoln's assassination**

▼ **This poster announced the rewards for capturing Booth and his group.**

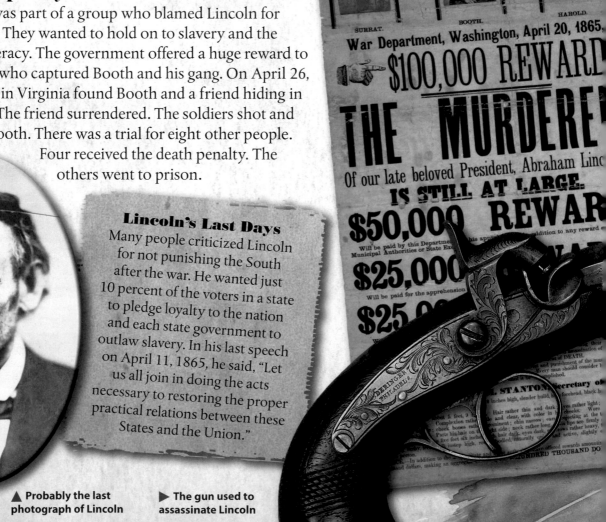

FORD'S THEAT
FRIDAY.
Dress Ci
Section......
No......

SURRAT.   BOOTH.   HAROLD.

War Department, Washington, April 20, 1865,

$100,000 REWARD

THE MURDERE

Of our late beloved President, Abraham Linc

IS STILL AT LARGE.

$50,000 REWAR

Will be paid by this Department ... this appr ... oldition to any reward ...
Municipal Authorities or State Exe

$25,000

Will be paid for the apprehension

$25,0

Lincoln's Last Days

Many people criticized Lincoln for not punishing the South after the war. He wanted just 10 percent of the voters in a state to pledge loyalty to the nation and each state government to outlaw slavery. In his last speech on April 11, 1865, he said, "Let us all join in doing the acts necessary to restoring the proper practical relations between these States and the Union."

▲ **Probably the last photograph of Lincoln**

▶ **The gun used to assassinate Lincoln**

► As Abraham Lincoln lay slumped over the rail of the theater box mortally wounded, Booth jumped onto the stage, breaking his leg in the fall, and limped away. Before he jumped, he stabbed a man who tried to tackle him.

Lincoln's Funeral

Lincoln's assassination brought shock and grief to the nation. His body was put on public display in the White House and the Capitol. Crowds lined up to view their president one last time. Then the body was taken by train from Washington, D.C., to Springfield, Illinois, one of Lincoln's hometowns. The trip lasted 13 days. Thousands of people lined the railroad tracks and wept as the train passed. In Chicago, officials displayed the body in the county courthouse. The burial took place in Oak Ridge Cemetery, Springfield. There is a monument at his tomb.

◄ President Lincoln's body was carried in this hearse to Oak Ridge Cemetery.

The Confederate president

During the war, Confederate President Jefferson Davis lived in the capital of Richmond. He met with the Confederate Congress and managed his military leaders. Just before Lee surrendered, Davis fled from Richmond. He encouraged a few more small battles in the South, but those ended on May 26, 1865.

Davis wanted to escape to Texas to start a new Confederacy. However, U.S. soldiers captured him in Georgia and took him to Fort Monroe, Virginia. He was accused of treason and Lincoln's assassination. There was never a trial, although he sat in prison for two years. After that, he spent the rest of his life on his plantation in Mississippi. He wrote books and gave speeches. Jefferson Davis died on December 6, 1889.

Reconstruction
Shattered lives begin again

The Civil War changed the nation. Many people wanted to rebuild their cities and farms, mend the government, and help former slaves start a new life. The job was harder than expected.

With Lincoln's death, vice president Andrew Johnson became the president. He started the period of rebuilding known as Reconstruction. President Johnson and Congress argued about it. The president was more generous about letting southern states back into the Union. Congress was more generous in giving African Americans the right to vote. In the end, Congress's plan won.

The U.S. Army was put in charge of each southern state until it followed new rules. Anyone who supported the Confederacy could not vote or hold office in the new state government. This included Confederate soldiers. The state also had to approve the 14th Amendment, which said that, as U.S. citizens, African Americans would receive "equal protection under the law."

President on Trial

In their arguments about Reconstruction, Congress passed laws to limit President Johnson's power. Johnson ignored these laws. In 1869, Congress impeached him. That means they put him on trial for wrongdoing. But there were not enough votes in Congress to remove him from office.

Victory Day

President Johnson announced the end of the war on May 10, 1865. In the two-day Victory Parade, Generals Meade and Sherman brought their troops (145,000 soldiers in all) to Washington, D.C. They cleaned up their uniforms and shined their shoes before marching proudly through the city. Johnson and General-in-chief Grant stood in front of the White House to watch it all. Sherman later said, "It was the happiest and most satisfactory moment of my life."

◀ The Victory Parade in Washington, D.C., on May 23 and 24, 1865

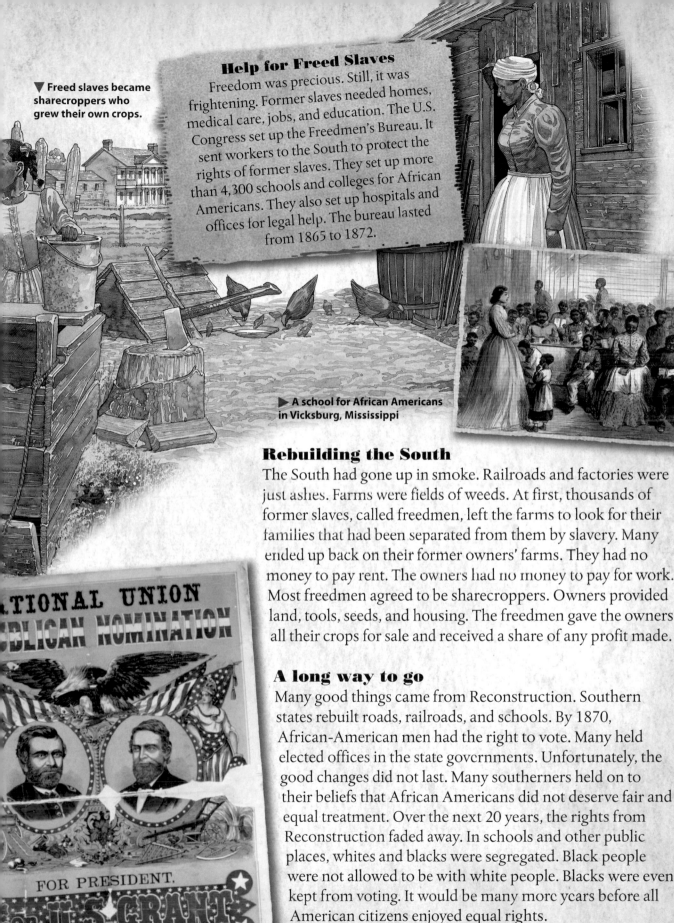

▼ Freed slaves became sharecroppers who grew their own crops.

Help for Freed Slaves

Freedom was precious. Still, it was frightening. Former slaves needed homes, medical care, jobs, and education. The U.S. Congress set up the Freedmen's Bureau. It sent workers to the South to protect the rights of former slaves. They set up more than 4,300 schools and colleges for African Americans. They also set up hospitals and offices for legal help. The bureau lasted from 1865 to 1872.

▶ A school for African Americans in Vicksburg, Mississippi

Rebuilding the South

The South had gone up in smoke. Railroads and factories were just ashes. Farms were fields of weeds. At first, thousands of former slaves, called freedmen, left the farms to look for their families that had been separated from them by slavery. Many ended up back on their former owners' farms. They had no money to pay rent. The owners had no money to pay for work. Most freedmen agreed to be sharecroppers. Owners provided land, tools, seeds, and housing. The freedmen gave the owners all their crops for sale and received a share of any profit made.

A long way to go

Many good things came from Reconstruction. Southern states rebuilt roads, railroads, and schools. By 1870, African-American men had the right to vote. Many held elected offices in the state governments. Unfortunately, the good changes did not last. Many southerners held on to their beliefs that African Americans did not deserve fair and equal treatment. Over the next 20 years, the rights from Reconstruction faded away. In schools and other public places, whites and blacks were segregated. Black people were not allowed to be with white people. Blacks were even kept from voting. It would be many more years before all American citizens enjoyed equal rights.

NATIONAL UNION
EPUBLICAN NOMINATION

FOR PRESIDENT.
Gen. U.S. GRANT

FOR VICE PRESIDENT.
SCHUYLER COLFAX

◀ This is a poster from the presidential election of 1868. General Ulysses S. Grant won the election.

Glossary

abolitionist someone who worked to end slavery

amendment a change to a document

assassination the murder of someone who is well known, such as the president

blockade something that stops goods or people from moving

candidate someone who is running in an election, competing for votes

capital city where the government of a state or country is located

Civil War (1861–1865) in the United States, the war between the northern and southern states

compromise an agreement in which both sides give up something and gain something

Confederacy the group of southern states that left the U.S. during the Civil War

Congress the branch of U.S. government that makes laws

conspiracy a secret plan made by two or more people to take over or bring an end to something

draft to make someone join the armed forces, such as the army or navy

Emancipation Proclamation an order that freed the slaves in Confederate states

factory a building where things are made using machines

fort a strong building that can protect people from attacks

freedman a former slave who is free

fugitive someone who escapes from the law

government the group of people who run a country or state

immigrant someone who arrives in a country from a different country

inauguration a ceremony to put someone in office, such as a country's president

ironclad a strong ship that is protected with a covering of iron plates

plantation a large farm where cotton and tobacco are often grown. A person who owns a plantation is called a planter

Reconstruction the period following the Civil War when former slaves were given rights and new people in government tried to rebuild the South

representative a person chosen to speak or act for others

right something that the law says a person can do or have

secede to leave a group, usually to form another group

sharecropper someone who farms land for another person and is a paid a share of the income from selling the crops

siege the surrounding of a city in order to cut off supplies to it

slave someone who is owned by another person and is made to work for that person

surrender to give up or admit that you cannot win

territory in the United States, an area that belongs to the nation but is not a state

treason the crime of hurting your country by helping an enemy

Underground Railroad secret routes that helped runaway slaves escape to free states and Canada

Union the United States of America

Yankee a person who fought for the Union in the Civil War

Timeline

1850 Congress passes Compromise of 1850 and
Fugitive Slave Act
1859 John Brown attempts slave rebellion at Harpers
Ferry, Virginia
1860 Lincoln wins presidential election; South Carolina
is first of 11 states to secede from the Union

1861
April 12 Civil War begins as Confederates fire on Fort
Sumter, South Carolina
April 19 Lincoln orders a naval blockade of the South
July 21 Battle of Bull Run

1862
March 9 Battle of the *Monitor* and the *Virginia*
May–June McClellan's failed Richmond campaign
September 17 Battle of Antietam
December 11–15 Battle of Fredericksburg

1863
January 1 Lincoln's Emancipation Proclamation
July 1–3 Battle of Gettysburg
July 4 Union wins long battle at Vicksburg, Mississippi
July 13 New York draft riots begin
November 19 Lincoln's Gettysburg Address

1864
March 9 Grant made general-in-chief of the Union army
June Start of Union's nine-month siege of Petersburg
September 2 Sherman's Union troops capture Atlanta
November 8 Lincoln is re-elected president
November 15 Sherman begins his final onslaught

1865
February 6 Lee made general-in-chief of the
Confederates
April 2 The fall of Richmond
April 9 Lee surrenders to Grant at Appomattox Court
House
April 14 Lincoln is assassinated
May 26 Last Confederate troops surrender
December 6 13th Amendment ends slavery

Information

WEBSITES
Aboard the Underground Railroad
**www.nps.gov/history/nr/travel/underground/
ugrrintr.htm**

Civil War Traveler
Links to battle sites
www.civilwartraveler.com

Encyclopedia Virginia
Search for topics such as "John Brown" or "Civil War"
www.encyclopediavirginia.org

Gettysburg National Military Park
www.nps.gov/gett/index.htm

Library of Congress—the Civil War
**www.americaslibrary.gov/jb/civil/jb_civil_
subj.html**

Lincoln's Gettysburg Address
**www.ourdocuments.gov/doc.php?flash=
old&doc=36**

BOOKS TO READ
Allen, Thomas B. and Roger MacBride Allen.
Mr. Lincoln's High-Tech War. Washington, DC:
National Geographic, 2009.
Hart, Alison. *Gabriel's Journey.* Atlanta: Peachtree
Publishers, 2007.
Hopkinson, Deborah, and Brian Floca. *Billy and the
Rebel: Based on a True Civil War Story.* New York:
Atheneum Books for Young Readers, 2005.
Marsico, Katie. *Great Battles of the Civil War.* Vero
Beach, FL: Rourke Publishing, 2010.
Sheinkin, Steve, and Tim Robinson. *Two Miserable
Presidents: Everything Your Schoolbooks Didn't Tell
You About the Civil War.* New York: Roaring Brook
Press, 2008.
Todras, Ellen H. *The Gettysburg Battlefield.* New York:
Chelsea Clubhouse, 2010.

Index

continued from the front page

And I hereby enjoin upon the people so declared to be free to abstain from all violence, unless in necessary self-defence; and I recommend to them that, in all cases when allowed, they labor faithfully for reasonable wages.

And I further declare and make known, that such persons of suitable condition, will be received into the armed service of the United States to garrison forts, positions, stations, and other places, and to man vessels of all sorts in said service.

And upon this act, sincerely believed to be an act of justice, warranted by the Constitution, upon military necessity, I invoke the considerate judgment of mankind, and the gracious favor of Almighty God.

In witness whereof, I have hereunto set my hand and caused the seal of the United States to be affixed.

Done at the City of Washington, this first day of January, in the year of our Lord one thousand eight hundred and sixty three, and of the Independence of the United States of America the eighty-seventh.

By the President: ABRAHAM LINCOLN
WILLIAM H. SEWARD, Secretary of State.

The Gettysburg Address

Four score and seven years ago our fathers brought forth on this continent a new nation conceived in liberty and dedicated to the proposition that all men are created equal.

Now we are engaged in a great civil war testing whether that nation or any nation so conceived and so dedicated can long endure. We are met on a great battlefield of that war. We have come to dedicate a portion of that field as a final resting place for those who here gave their lives that that nation might live. It is altogether fitting and proper that we should do this. But in a larger sense we can not dedicate—we can not consecrate— we can not hallow—this ground. The brave men living and dead who struggled here have consecrated it far above our poor power to add or detract. The world will little note nor long remember what we say here but it can never forget what they did here. It is for us the living rather to be dedicated here to the unfinished work which they who fought here have thus far so nobly advanced. It is rather for us to be here dedicated to the great task remaining before us—that from these honored dead we take increased devotion to that cause for which they gave the last full measure of devotion—that we here highly resolve that these dead shall not have died in vain—that this nation under God shall have a new birth of freedom—and that government of the people by the people for the people shall not perish from the earth.

Abraham Lincoln
November 19, 1863

Note: this transcription of the Gettysburg Address reflects the version inscribed on the wall of the Lincoln Memorial in Washington, D.C., which is based on Lincoln's final known handwritten draft, called the Bliss copy.
Source for Emancipation Proclamation text: www.ourdocuments.gov